50 Mexican Burrito and Taco Recipes

By: Kelly Johnson

Table of Contents

- Carne Asada Tacos
- Chicken Tinga Tacos
- Carnitas Burritos
- Al Pastor Tacos
- Barbacoa Tacos
- Veggie Burritos
- Baja Fish Tacos
- Shrimp Tacos with Lime Crema
- Chorizo and Potato Tacos
- Breakfast Burritos
- Chipotle Chicken Burritos
- Pork Belly Tacos
- Beef Picadillo Burritos
- Black Bean and Corn Tacos
- Fajita Burritos
- Turkey Tacos with Avocado
- Pulled Pork Tacos
- Mushroom Tacos
- Grilled Chicken Burritos
- Sinaloa-Style Shrimp Tacos
- Bean and Cheese Burritos
- Slow Cooker Beef Tacos
- Crispy Tacos Dorados
- Steak and Guacamole Burritos
- Duck Carnitas Tacos
- Veggie Tacos with Roasted Vegetables
- Ground Beef and Cheese Tacos
- Chipotle Pork Burritos
- Tacos al Carbon
- Chicken Mole Tacos
- Lamb Barbacoa Burritos
- Fish Tacos with Mango Salsa
- Chile Relleno Burritos
- Jackfruit Tacos
- Pork and Pineapple Tacos

- Carne Seca Burritos
- Soft Chicken Tacos
- Spicy Shrimp Burritos
- Chicken and Black Bean Tacos
- Beef Brisket Tacos
- Zucchini and Corn Tacos
- Spicy Chicken Burritos
- Grilled Steak Tacos with Salsa Verde
- Chicken Adobo Tacos
- Pork Verde Burritos
- Cauliflower Tacos with Chipotle Crema
- Short Rib Tacos
- Grilled Veggie Burritos
- Queso Fundido Tacos
- BBQ Pork Burritos

Carne Asada Tacos

Ingredients:

- 1 lb skirt steak or flank steak
- 1 tablespoon olive oil
- 1 teaspoon cumin
- 1 teaspoon chili powder
- 1/2 teaspoon garlic powder
- Salt and pepper to taste
- Corn tortillas
- Fresh cilantro, chopped
- Lime wedges

Instructions:

1. Season the steak with olive oil, cumin, chili powder, garlic powder, salt, and pepper.
2. Grill or sear the steak to desired doneness.
3. Let the steak rest, then slice thinly.
4. Serve on warmed corn tortillas and garnish with cilantro and lime wedges.

Chicken Tinga Tacos

Ingredients:

- 2 lbs chicken breast, cooked and shredded
- 1 tablespoon olive oil
- 1 onion, sliced
- 2 cloves garlic, minced
- 1 can chipotle peppers in adobo sauce
- 1 can diced tomatoes
- 1 teaspoon cumin
- Corn tortillas
- Fresh cilantro, chopped
- Lime wedges

Instructions:

1. Sauté onions and garlic in olive oil until softened.
2. Add chipotle peppers, diced tomatoes, cumin, and shredded chicken.
3. Simmer for 20 minutes, allowing the flavors to combine.
4. Serve on warmed tortillas with cilantro and lime.

Carnitas Burritos

Ingredients:

- 2 lbs pork shoulder, cut into chunks
- 1 tablespoon olive oil
- 1 onion, chopped
- 2 cloves garlic, minced
- 1 teaspoon cumin
- 1 cup chicken broth
- Flour tortillas
- Shredded lettuce
- Guacamole
- Sour cream

Instructions:

1. Brown the pork chunks in olive oil, then sauté onions and garlic.
2. Add cumin, chicken broth, and simmer for 2-3 hours until pork is tender.
3. Shred the pork and assemble in burritos with lettuce, guacamole, and sour cream.

Al Pastor Tacos

Ingredients:

- 1 lb pork shoulder, thinly sliced
- 2 tablespoons achiote paste
- 1/2 cup pineapple juice
- 1 teaspoon cumin
- 1/2 onion, sliced
- Corn tortillas
- Pineapple chunks
- Cilantro, chopped
- Lime wedges

Instructions:

1. Marinate pork slices with achiote paste, pineapple juice, cumin, and salt for 1 hour.
2. Grill or cook the pork until charred, then slice thinly.
3. Serve on tortillas with grilled pineapple, cilantro, and lime.

Barbacoa Tacos

Ingredients:

- 2 lbs beef chuck roast
- 1 onion, chopped
- 3 cloves garlic, minced
- 2 teaspoons cumin
- 1 teaspoon oregano
- 1 tablespoon vinegar
- 1 cup beef broth
- Corn tortillas
- Fresh cilantro, chopped
- Lime wedges

Instructions:

1. Brown beef chuck in a pot, then add onions, garlic, cumin, oregano, vinegar, and beef broth.
2. Simmer for 3-4 hours until the beef is tender and shreds easily.
3. Serve on tortillas with cilantro and lime.

Veggie Burritos

Ingredients:

- 1 cup black beans, cooked
- 1 cup corn kernels
- 1 red bell pepper, chopped
- 1/2 onion, chopped
- 1 tablespoon olive oil
- Flour tortillas
- Guacamole
- Sour cream

Instructions:

1. Sauté bell pepper, onion, and corn in olive oil until tender.
2. Heat the beans and combine with sautéed vegetables.
3. Assemble the burritos with the veggie mix, guacamole, and sour cream.

Baja Fish Tacos

Ingredients:

- 1 lb white fish fillets (such as cod or tilapia)
- 1/2 cup flour
- 1/2 teaspoon paprika
- 1/2 teaspoon garlic powder
- 1 teaspoon salt
- 1 teaspoon black pepper
- 1/2 cup cornmeal
- Corn tortillas
- Cabbage slaw
- Lime wedges

Instructions:

1. Coat fish fillets in flour, paprika, garlic powder, salt, and pepper.
2. Fry the fish in hot oil until golden and crispy.
3. Serve on tortillas with cabbage slaw and lime wedges.

Shrimp Tacos with Lime Crema

Ingredients:

- 1 lb shrimp, peeled and deveined
- 1 tablespoon olive oil
- 1 teaspoon chili powder
- 1/2 teaspoon cumin
- 1/2 cup sour cream
- 2 tablespoons lime juice
- Corn tortillas
- Fresh cilantro, chopped

Instructions:

1. Sauté shrimp in olive oil with chili powder and cumin until cooked.
2. Mix sour cream with lime juice to make lime crema.
3. Serve shrimp on tortillas with a drizzle of lime crema and cilantro.

Chorizo and Potato Tacos

Ingredients:

- 1 lb chorizo sausage, crumbled
- 2 medium potatoes, diced and cooked
- 1/2 onion, chopped
- Corn tortillas
- Fresh cilantro, chopped

Instructions:

1. Cook the chorizo until browned, then add onions and cook until softened.
2. Add cooked potatoes and mix well.
3. Serve on tortillas with cilantro.

Breakfast Burritos

Ingredients:

- 4 eggs, scrambled
- 1/2 cup cooked breakfast sausage or bacon
- 1/4 cup shredded cheese (cheddar or Monterey Jack)
- 1/4 cup sautéed bell peppers and onions
- Flour tortillas
- Salsa or hot sauce (optional)

Instructions:

1. Scramble the eggs and cook the sausage or bacon.
2. Sauté the bell peppers and onions until soft.
3. Assemble the burrito with scrambled eggs, sausage or bacon, sautéed veggies, and cheese.
4. Roll up in a flour tortilla and serve with salsa or hot sauce if desired.

Chipotle Chicken Burritos

Ingredients:

- 2 chicken breasts, grilled and sliced
- 1 tablespoon chipotle in adobo sauce
- 1 teaspoon cumin
- 1/2 cup rice, cooked
- 1/4 cup black beans
- 1/4 cup shredded cheese
- Sour cream
- Flour tortillas

Instructions:

1. Marinate grilled chicken in chipotle, adobo sauce, and cumin.
2. Layer the cooked rice, black beans, and marinated chicken in a tortilla.
3. Add cheese and sour cream before wrapping the burrito.

Pork Belly Tacos

Ingredients:

- 1 lb pork belly, cooked and sliced
- 1 tablespoon olive oil
- 1 teaspoon chili powder
- 1/2 teaspoon cumin
- Corn tortillas
- Cabbage slaw
- Lime wedges

Instructions:

1. Sear the cooked pork belly slices in olive oil with chili powder and cumin.
2. Serve the pork belly on corn tortillas, topped with cabbage slaw and a squeeze of lime.

Beef Picadillo Burritos

Ingredients:

- 1 lb ground beef
- 1 onion, chopped
- 1/2 cup diced potatoes
- 1/4 cup raisins
- 1/4 cup olives, chopped
- 1 teaspoon cumin
- 1 tablespoon tomato paste
- Flour tortillas
- Shredded lettuce

Instructions:

1. Brown the ground beef, then add onions and cook until softened.
2. Add diced potatoes, raisins, olives, cumin, and tomato paste. Simmer until potatoes are tender.
3. Fill burritos with the picadillo mixture and shredded lettuce.

Black Bean and Corn Tacos

Ingredients:

- 1 can black beans, drained and rinsed
- 1 cup corn kernels, cooked
- 1/2 onion, chopped
- 1 teaspoon cumin
- Corn tortillas
- Fresh cilantro, chopped
- Lime wedges

Instructions:

1. Sauté onions in a pan until softened, then add black beans, corn, and cumin. Cook for a few more minutes.
2. Serve the bean and corn mixture on warm corn tortillas, topped with cilantro and a squeeze of lime.

Fajita Burritos

Ingredients:

- 1 lb steak or chicken, thinly sliced
- 1 bell pepper, sliced
- 1 onion, sliced
- 1 tablespoon fajita seasoning
- 1 cup rice, cooked
- Flour tortillas
- Sour cream or guacamole

Instructions:

1. Sauté the meat with fajita seasoning until cooked through.
2. Add bell pepper and onion to the skillet and cook until tender.
3. Assemble burritos with the fajita mixture, rice, and sour cream or guacamole.

Turkey Tacos with Avocado

Ingredients:

- 1 lb ground turkey
- 1 teaspoon cumin
- 1 tablespoon chili powder
- 1/4 cup water
- Corn tortillas
- 1 avocado, sliced
- Fresh cilantro, chopped
- Lime wedges

Instructions:

1. Brown the ground turkey and cook with cumin, chili powder, and water until the turkey is cooked through and the flavors have melded.
2. Serve in tortillas with avocado slices, cilantro, and a squeeze of lime.

Pulled Pork Tacos

Ingredients:

- 2 lbs pork shoulder, cooked and shredded
- 1/4 cup barbecue sauce
- 1/2 onion, chopped
- Corn tortillas
- Pickled jalapeños
- Fresh cilantro, chopped

Instructions:

1. Mix the shredded pork with barbecue sauce.
2. Serve the pulled pork on tortillas and top with onions, pickled jalapeños, and cilantro.

Mushroom Tacos

Ingredients:

- 1 lb mushrooms, sliced
- 1 tablespoon olive oil
- 1 teaspoon garlic powder
- Corn tortillas
- Fresh cilantro, chopped
- Lime wedges

Instructions:

1. Sauté the sliced mushrooms in olive oil with garlic powder until tender.
2. Serve the mushrooms on corn tortillas and top with cilantro and a squeeze of lime.

Grilled Chicken Burritos

Ingredients:

- 2 chicken breasts, grilled and sliced
- 1/2 cup cooked rice
- 1/4 cup black beans
- 1/4 cup shredded cheese
- Salsa or guacamole
- Flour tortillas

Instructions:

1. Grill the chicken breasts and slice them into strips.
2. Assemble the burrito by layering rice, black beans, grilled chicken, shredded cheese, and salsa or guacamole in a flour tortilla.
3. Roll up and serve!

Sinaloa-Style Shrimp Tacos

Ingredients:

- 1 lb shrimp, peeled and deveined
- 1 tablespoon chili powder
- 1/2 teaspoon paprika
- 1 teaspoon cumin
- 1 tablespoon olive oil
- Corn tortillas
- Cabbage slaw
- Lime wedges

Instructions:

1. Toss the shrimp in chili powder, paprika, cumin, and olive oil.
2. Cook the shrimp in a pan until pink and cooked through.
3. Serve the shrimp on warm corn tortillas, topped with cabbage slaw and a squeeze of lime.

Bean and Cheese Burritos

Ingredients:

- 1 can refried beans
- 1/4 cup shredded cheese (cheddar or Monterey Jack)
- 1/4 cup sour cream
- Flour tortillas
- Salsa (optional)

Instructions:

1. Heat the refried beans and place them in a warm flour tortilla.
2. Top with shredded cheese, sour cream, and salsa if desired.
3. Roll up the tortilla and serve.

Slow Cooker Beef Tacos

Ingredients:

- 2 lbs beef chuck roast
- 1 packet taco seasoning
- 1/2 cup beef broth
- Corn tortillas
- Shredded lettuce
- Salsa

Instructions:

1. Place the beef roast in a slow cooker with taco seasoning and beef broth.
2. Cook on low for 8 hours or high for 4 hours.
3. Shred the beef and serve in warm corn tortillas with shredded lettuce and salsa.

Crispy Tacos Dorados

Ingredients:

- 2 cups cooked ground beef or chicken
- 1/4 cup diced onions
- Corn tortillas
- Vegetable oil (for frying)
- Shredded cheese
- Sour cream

Instructions:

1. Heat oil in a pan and lightly fry the corn tortillas to make them crispy.
2. Fill the crispy tortillas with ground beef or chicken and top with diced onions and shredded cheese.
3. Serve with sour cream on the side.

Steak and Guacamole Burritos

Ingredients:

- 1 lb steak, grilled and sliced
- 1/4 cup guacamole
- 1/2 cup cooked rice
- 1/4 cup shredded cheese
- Flour tortillas

Instructions:

1. Grill the steak and slice it into strips.
2. Assemble the burrito by layering rice, steak, guacamole, and shredded cheese in a flour tortilla.
3. Roll up the burrito and serve!

Duck Carnitas Tacos

Ingredients:

- 2 duck legs
- 1 tablespoon cumin
- 1 tablespoon chili powder
- 1/2 cup orange juice
- Corn tortillas
- Shredded cabbage
- Salsa verde

Instructions:

1. Cook the duck legs in a slow cooker with cumin, chili powder, and orange juice until tender (about 4 hours on low).
2. Shred the duck meat and serve in corn tortillas with shredded cabbage and salsa verde.

Veggie Tacos with Roasted Vegetables

Ingredients:

- 1 zucchini, sliced
- 1 bell pepper, sliced
- 1 onion, sliced
- 1 teaspoon cumin
- 1 tablespoon olive oil
- Corn tortillas
- Fresh cilantro
- Lime wedges

Instructions:

1. Toss the zucchini, bell pepper, and onion in olive oil and cumin, then roast at 400°F for 20-25 minutes.
2. Serve the roasted vegetables in corn tortillas, topped with fresh cilantro and a squeeze of lime.

Ground Beef and Cheese Tacos

Ingredients:

- 1 lb ground beef
- 1 packet taco seasoning
- Corn tortillas
- Shredded cheese
- Lettuce, chopped

Instructions:

1. Cook the ground beef and add taco seasoning.
2. Serve the beef in corn tortillas, topped with shredded cheese and chopped lettuce.

Chipotle Pork Burritos

Ingredients:

- 1 lb pork shoulder, shredded
- 2 tablespoons chipotle peppers in adobo sauce
- 1/4 cup orange juice
- 1 tablespoon garlic, minced
- Flour tortillas
- Rice, beans, shredded cheese

Instructions:

1. Cook the pork shoulder with chipotle peppers, orange juice, and garlic in a slow cooker for 6-8 hours or until tender.
2. Shred the pork and assemble the burritos by adding rice, beans, shredded cheese, and the chipotle pork in a flour tortilla.
3. Roll up and serve!

Tacos al Carbon

Ingredients:

- 1 lb skirt steak or flank steak
- 1 tablespoon lime juice
- 1 tablespoon garlic, minced
- Corn tortillas
- Chopped cilantro, onions, salsa

Instructions:

1. Marinate the steak in lime juice and garlic for 30 minutes.
2. Grill the steak over high heat until cooked to your liking, then slice thinly.
3. Serve the steak in warm corn tortillas with chopped cilantro, onions, and salsa.

Chicken Mole Tacos

Ingredients:

- 2 chicken breasts, shredded
- 1/2 cup mole sauce
- Corn tortillas
- Chopped onions, cilantro, and queso fresco

Instructions:

1. Cook the chicken and shred it. Mix it with mole sauce and heat until warm.
2. Serve the mole chicken in corn tortillas, topped with onions, cilantro, and crumbled queso fresco.

Lamb Barbacoa Burritos

Ingredients:

- 1 lb lamb shoulder, cooked and shredded
- 2 tablespoons adobo sauce
- 1/4 cup beef broth
- Flour tortillas
- Rice, beans, salsa, and cilantro

Instructions:

1. Slow cook the lamb shoulder with adobo sauce and beef broth for 6-8 hours until tender.
2. Shred the lamb and assemble the burritos by adding rice, beans, salsa, and lamb in a flour tortilla.
3. Roll up and serve!

Fish Tacos with Mango Salsa

Ingredients:

- 1 lb white fish fillets (such as cod or tilapia)
- 1 tablespoon cumin
- 1 tablespoon paprika
- 1/2 cup mango, diced
- 1/4 cup red onion, diced
- Corn tortillas

Instructions:

1. Season the fish with cumin and paprika, then cook in a skillet until flaky.
2. Mix the mango and red onion to create the salsa.
3. Serve the fish in corn tortillas, topped with mango salsa.

Chile Relleno Burritos

Ingredients:

- 2 large poblano peppers
- 1 lb ground beef
- 1/4 cup shredded cheese
- 1/2 cup tomato sauce
- Flour tortillas

Instructions:

1. Roast the poblano peppers and remove the skin.
2. Stuff the peppers with ground beef and shredded cheese, then top with tomato sauce.
3. Wrap the stuffed peppers in a flour tortilla to form a burrito.

Jackfruit Tacos

Ingredients:

- 1 can young green jackfruit, shredded
- 1 tablespoon soy sauce
- 1 teaspoon cumin
- 1/4 cup onions, diced
- Corn tortillas

Instructions:

1. Sauté the jackfruit with soy sauce and cumin until tender and slightly caramelized.
2. Serve the jackfruit in warm corn tortillas, topped with diced onions.

Pork and Pineapple Tacos

Ingredients:

- 1 lb pork shoulder, shredded
- 1 cup pineapple, diced
- 1 tablespoon chili powder
- Corn tortillas
- Cilantro and lime wedges

Instructions:

1. Cook the pork shoulder until tender, then shred it.
2. Toss the shredded pork with diced pineapple and chili powder.
3. Serve in corn tortillas, topped with fresh cilantro and a squeeze of lime.

Carne Seca Burritos

Ingredients:

- 1 lb beef jerky (carne seca), shredded
- 1/4 cup beef broth
- Flour tortillas
- Refried beans, rice, salsa, and cheese

Instructions:

1. Soak the carne seca in beef broth to soften it, then shred it.
2. Assemble the burritos by adding refried beans, rice, cheese, salsa, and carne seca in a flour tortilla.
3. Roll up and serve!

Soft Chicken Tacos

Ingredients:

- 2 chicken breasts, cooked and shredded
- 1 tablespoon taco seasoning
- 8 small flour tortillas
- Lettuce, tomatoes, shredded cheese, and salsa

Instructions:

1. Cook the chicken breasts and shred them.
2. Toss the chicken in taco seasoning and heat through.
3. Warm the tortillas and fill them with the seasoned chicken.
4. Top with lettuce, tomatoes, shredded cheese, and salsa.

Spicy Shrimp Burritos

Ingredients:

- 1 lb shrimp, peeled and deveined
- 1 tablespoon chili powder
- 1 tablespoon paprika
- 1/2 cup sour cream
- Flour tortillas
- Rice, lettuce, and salsa

Instructions:

1. Season the shrimp with chili powder and paprika, then sauté them until cooked through.
2. In a flour tortilla, add a layer of rice, then top with shrimp, lettuce, and salsa.
3. Drizzle with sour cream and roll up the burrito.

Chicken and Black Bean Tacos

Ingredients:

- 2 chicken breasts, cooked and shredded
- 1 can black beans, drained and rinsed
- 1 teaspoon cumin
- 8 soft corn tortillas
- Chopped cilantro, onions, and salsa

Instructions:

1. Cook and shred the chicken, then mix with black beans and cumin.
2. Warm the tortillas and fill with the chicken and black bean mixture.
3. Top with cilantro, onions, and salsa.

Beef Brisket Tacos

Ingredients:

- 1 lb beef brisket, slow-cooked and shredded
- 1 tablespoon chili powder
- 1 teaspoon cumin
- Corn tortillas
- Onions, cilantro, and lime wedges

Instructions:

1. Slow-cook the brisket with chili powder and cumin until tender, then shred it.
2. Serve the shredded brisket in warm corn tortillas.
3. Top with onions, cilantro, and a squeeze of lime.

Zucchini and Corn Tacos

Ingredients:

- 2 zucchinis, chopped
- 1 cup corn kernels
- 1 teaspoon cumin
- 8 small corn tortillas
- Feta cheese and cilantro

Instructions:

1. Sauté the zucchini and corn with cumin until tender.
2. Warm the tortillas and fill with the zucchini and corn mixture.
3. Top with crumbled feta cheese and fresh cilantro.

Spicy Chicken Burritos

Ingredients:

- 2 chicken breasts, cooked and shredded
- 1 tablespoon chipotle chili powder
- 1/2 cup salsa
- Flour tortillas
- Rice, beans, shredded cheese, and guacamole

Instructions:

1. Shred the cooked chicken and toss it with chipotle chili powder and salsa.
2. In a flour tortilla, layer rice, beans, shredded cheese, and the spicy chicken mixture.
3. Add guacamole, roll up, and serve.

Grilled Steak Tacos with Salsa Verde

Ingredients:

- 1 lb flank steak, grilled and sliced
- 1/2 cup salsa verde
- 8 small corn tortillas
- Chopped onions, cilantro, and lime wedges

Instructions:

1. Grill the steak and slice it thinly.
2. Warm the tortillas and fill them with the sliced steak.
3. Top with salsa verde, chopped onions, cilantro, and a squeeze of lime.

Chicken Adobo Tacos

Ingredients:

- 2 chicken thighs, cooked and shredded
- 1/4 cup adobo sauce
- 8 corn tortillas
- Pickled red onions, cilantro, and lime wedges

Instructions:

1. Shred the cooked chicken and mix with adobo sauce.
2. Warm the tortillas and fill with the chicken adobo.
3. Top with pickled red onions, cilantro, and a squeeze of lime.

Pork Verde Burritos

Ingredients:

- 1 lb pork shoulder, slow-cooked and shredded
- 1/2 cup green salsa
- Flour tortillas
- Rice, beans, and cheese

Instructions:

1. Slow-cook the pork shoulder until tender, then shred it.
2. Mix the shredded pork with green salsa.
3. Assemble the burritos by adding rice, beans, cheese, and the pork verde mixture in a flour tortilla.
4. Roll up and serve.

Cauliflower Tacos with Chipotle Crema

Ingredients:

- 1 head of cauliflower, chopped into florets
- 2 tablespoons olive oil
- 1 teaspoon cumin
- 1 teaspoon chili powder
- 1/2 cup chipotle crema (mix sour cream with chipotle chili in adobo)
- 8 small corn tortillas
- Fresh cilantro, lime wedges, and sliced radishes

Instructions:

1. Toss the cauliflower florets in olive oil, cumin, and chili powder. Roast at 400°F (200°C) for 25-30 minutes until crispy.
2. Warm the tortillas and fill with the roasted cauliflower.
3. Drizzle with chipotle crema and top with fresh cilantro, lime wedges, and sliced radishes.

Short Rib Tacos

Ingredients:

- 1 lb beef short ribs
- 1 tablespoon taco seasoning
- 1 onion, sliced
- 2 garlic cloves, minced
- 8 soft corn tortillas
- Cilantro, pickled red onions, and salsa

Instructions:

1. Season the short ribs with taco seasoning and brown in a pan.
2. Add the onions and garlic, then slow-cook the short ribs in a pot until tender (about 2-3 hours).
3. Shred the meat and serve in warm tortillas.
4. Top with cilantro, pickled red onions, and salsa.

Grilled Veggie Burritos

Ingredients:

- 1 zucchini, sliced
- 1 bell pepper, sliced
- 1 onion, sliced
- 1 tablespoon olive oil
- 1 cup rice
- Flour tortillas
- Guacamole, sour cream, and shredded cheese

Instructions:

1. Toss the sliced vegetables in olive oil and grill until tender.
2. Cook the rice according to package instructions.
3. Warm the tortillas and layer with rice, grilled vegetables, guacamole, sour cream, and shredded cheese.
4. Roll up the burritos and serve.

Queso Fundido Tacos

Ingredients:

- 1/2 lb chorizo sausage, cooked
- 2 cups shredded Oaxaca cheese
- 8 small flour tortillas
- Cilantro, diced onions, and salsa

Instructions:

1. Cook the chorizo in a pan and set aside.
2. In the same pan, melt the shredded Oaxaca cheese until gooey.
3. Warm the tortillas and fill with chorizo and melted cheese.
4. Top with fresh cilantro, diced onions, and salsa.

BBQ Pork Burritos

Ingredients:

- 1 lb pork shoulder, slow-cooked and shredded
- 1/2 cup BBQ sauce
- Flour tortillas
- Rice, beans, shredded cheese, and pickled jalapeños

Instructions:

1. Slow-cook the pork shoulder until tender, then shred it.
2. Mix the shredded pork with BBQ sauce.
3. Warm the tortillas and layer with rice, beans, shredded cheese, and BBQ pork.
4. Add pickled jalapeños, roll up the burritos, and serve.

www.ingramcontent.com/pod-product-compliance
Lightning Source LLC
LaVergne TN
LVHW081342060526
838201LV00055B/2797